ALLEN CARR'S

NO MORE WORRYING

The Easy Way to a Worry-free Life

ARCTURUS

ARCTURUS

Arcturus Publishing Limited
26/27 Bickels Yard, 151–153 Bermondsey Street
London SE1 3HA

Published in association with
foulsham
W. Foulsham & Co. Ltd,
The Publishing House, Bennetts Close, Cippenham,
Slough, Berkshire SL1 5AP, England

ISBN 13: 978-0572-03185-5
ISBN 10: 0-572-03185-8

This edition printed in 2006

Text Copyright © 2006 Allen Carr's Easyway (International) Limited
Design Copyright © 2006 Arcturus Publishing Limited
Orginally published in 2003 as *Allen Carr's Easy Way to Stop Worrying*

British Library Cataloguing-in-Publication Data: a catalogue record for this book
is available from the British Library

Printed in England by J. H. Haynes & Co. Ltd, Nr Yeovil, Somerset

Typeset by MATS.

Cover design by Emma Avery

PREFACE

'When burdened with worry and life goes wrong, just buckle your armour and trudge along!'

From my earliest memories, this slogan, framed and handwritten in beautiful script, occupied the prime position above our fireplace. It was the quintessence of my mother's attitude to life: that the time spent on this earth is a penance.

And for her, it must have seemed that way. She was the eldest of fourteen children, her mother was an alcoholic and her father had deserted them. A child herself, she had successfully taken up the responsibility of being both mother and father to her siblings during the worst years of the depression.

There is no doubt whatsoever that my mother's attitude had a profound effect on me and my brothers and sister. My sister was least able to counteract the negative side of my mother's influence. She would say:

'My greatest worry is when I have nothing to worry about.'

This sounds like a contradiction: how can you worry when you have nothing to worry about? Yet I knew what she meant and I suspect you do, too! After all, when we have something to worry about, that worry obsesses our minds. If what we're worrying about actually happened, nine times out of ten it would be no tragedy. But that niggling worry, insignificant as it might be in itself, prevents us from worrying about real tragedies.

I've no doubt that being separated from my parents due to evacuation at the outbreak of World War Two merely confirmed the truth of the slogan for me. Winning a scholarship to a school at which every boy appeared to be socially, financially, physically and intellectually superior to me did nothing to disprove it. Nor did my chosen profession; I hated being an accountant.

As I look back on my life, it appeared to consist of only three things:

WORRY, WORRY AND WORRY!

There appeared to be just one bright side to my life: I had a truly great friend and companion, but for whom, I was convinced, I could not have handled these burdens. My friend was a packet of cigarettes. Not just one packet, you understand: I chain-smoked 60 to 100 cigarettes a day for over 30 years.

Needless to say, this friend had his faults. The biggest was that I knew he would kill me if I didn't give him up. I made several attempts to quit, but every time I was so miserable that I eventually found an excuse to start again. I took the attitude: if this is life without my friend, I'd rather have the shorter but happier life of the smoker.

In 1983 I discovered a method that would enable any smoker to quit immediately, easily and permanently, without using willpower or suffering withdrawal pangs. For obvious reasons I called it Easyway. I gave up being an accountant and eventually set up the first Easyway clinic. There are now over forty Easyway clinics throughout the world and I'm widely accepted as the world's leading expert on how to quit smoking.

It soon dawned on me that the Easyway method is more than just a cure for smoking and that it is just as effective for all drug addiction. In fact, it is a recipe for a happy life.

I'm trying to remember the last time I worried about something. It was 18 years ago, when I threw in my accountant's job and took on a £30,000 mortgage. I was worried that the Easyway venture might not be successful and that I would be unable to afford the mortgage on that first clinic. Given the same scenario today, I wouldn't have worried: not because in hindsight I was successful, but because there was no need to worry.

Am I categorically stating that I've never worried about a single matter since then? No, I am not. But the fact that I cannot remember worrying proves my point. I can remember that my whole life was one continual worry before I discovered Easyway.

Am I categorically stating that the remainder of my life will be completely free of worry, problems, depression and stress? No, I am not. I have many problems, but very rarely suffer from depression or stress.

This book is not a series of useful tips enabling you to cope with the worries of life better, but rather an explanation of why your life can be virtually

FREE FROM WORRY.

WAS I JUST LUCKY?

In the sense that, like most people, I had been brainwashed from birth to believe that worry is an unavoidable part of our lives and that I spent the bulk of what should have been the best years of my life in a constant state of worry, the answer is: no, I was decidedly unlucky! However, in the sense that I escaped from the brainwashing, whereas most people suffer it for life, I was exceedingly lucky!

WILL YOU NEED LUCK?

Fortunately, no! A person can spend a lifetime searching for the correct combination of a lock that will release them from prison. You can be released from the same prison in a matter of seconds merely by being told the correct combination.

WORRYING IS UNNATURAL

It is the result of brainwashing by civilized mankind. It took most of my life to discover the key that would release me from this prison. If you worry, you are in the same prison. The same key that released me will release you. Easyway is the key that will give you a worry-free life. To turn the key, all you need do is to follow the instructions.

OPEN YOUR MIND

This is the first and most important instruction; it also happens to be the most difficult. Do you think of yourself as an open-minded person? Of course you do, everybody does. Test it for yourself: try and find a single person who regards himself as narrow-minded. You won't find one! Therefore accept that you and I are the same.

IS THE EARTH ROUND OR FLAT?

If you live in England, do you visualize Australians standing upside down, or Spaniards sticking out from the side of the earth? For over 300 years, we've known that the earth moves round the sun and not vice versa. So why do we still visualize the sun rising in the East and setting in the West? These are two classic examples of knowing something, yet retaining a completely distorted view. With brainwashing, it is not only essential to remove the brainwashing, but also to remove the distorted view.

WHAT IS BRAINWASHING?

My dictionary defines it as: 'to effect a radical change in the ideas and beliefs of a person'. I accept that beauty is in the eyes of the beholder; but whether the world is round or flat is a question of fact. For the purposes of Easyway, I define brainwashing as 'convincing a person that a genuine fact is untrue'. Prior to 1492, people in the civilized world were brainwashed to believe that the world was flat. We have been brainwashed to believe that worrying is normal and inevitable. It is not.

ARE YOU CONVINCED THAT WORRYING IS INEVITABLE?

If so, you have already failed to follow the first instruction. Does this mean that I'm asking you to meekly accept everything I tell you without question? On the contrary, it is essential to be sceptical. Question what I tell you, also question your own beliefs and those society has led you to believe. All we are concerned with is to discover the truth. How can you claim to be open-minded if you start off with the preconception that worrying is inevitable?

IT'S NOT EASY TO BE OPEN-MINDED

It's easy to have a worry-free life if you understand and follow the instructions; but it's not always easy to follow the instructions. Can you imagine how difficult it was to convince people who had been brainwashed from birth to believe that the earth was flat, that it is in fact round, when everyone else believed it was flat and their own eyes could see it was flat? You are in a very similar position.

YOU HAVE ABSOLUTELY NOTHING TO LOSE

To question life-long beliefs takes both imagination and intelligence. It can also take courage, and that is what you are going to use. If you are reading a book on how to stop worrying, it is logical to assume that your life at present isn't all honey and roses and that you are probably feeling somewhat depressed. Don't! How often in life are you in a situation in which you have so much to gain and absolutely nothing to lose?

POSITIVE THINKING

Some believe that Easyway is merely an exercise in positive thinking. That is an essential ingredient and is **GOLDEN RULE NO. 1.** But there's much more to it than that. Positive thinking alone didn't enable me either to quit smoking or to be free from worry. You know the sort of thing: 'Always look on the bright side', or 'there's always someone worse off than you', or 'isn't it great to be alive?' Such techniques sound logical and actually help in certain circumstances. However, they can also be examples of:

NEGATIVE THINKING

Such advice is only offered when a tragedy has occurred, be it major or minor. It is designed to distract you from the tragedy. However, such thinking can actually be negative. Ostriches purportedly bury their heads in sand in the belief that if they cannot see danger – it doesn't exist. It is obvious that the ostrich is ten times more vulnerable with its head stuck in the sand. The examples I have given are common gambits that we use. Instead of addressing and solving a problem, we try to close our minds to it and hope it will solve itself, and by doing so we merely prolong and increase its effect. I was pleased to learn:

OSTRICHES DON'T STICK THEIR HEADS IN SAND

Neither do any of the other incredible variety of species on this planet. Why don't they do it? We've already answered that one: because it is an incredibly stupid thing to do. Do you not find it ironic that the only species on the planet that adopts such incredibly stupid tactics, is the species that in fact has the largest brain and believes itself to be the most intelligent, yet in reality:

IS LESS INTELLIGENT THAN
AN AMOEBA

How can this possibly be? Because every creature on this planet, including man, was created by Mother Nature. With the exception of ourselves, every species that has survived today has done so by acting on instinct: it has no choice but to follow the rules of Mother Nature. Those rules are based on natural selection: in other words, 3 billion years of trial and error.

HAVE I FORGOTTEN ABOUT GOD?

Not at all. But God means different things to different faiths. This book deals in fact not faith. Whichever God you happen to believe in, evolution was the process he or she used. We cannot deny his or her existence, so to avoid possible confusion or offence, I will refer only to Mother Nature.

AM I RELIGIOUS?

I cannot give a 'yes' or 'no' answer to this question. My dictionary defines religion as the 'belief in a supernatural power that has control over human destiny'. It defines supernatural as 'relative to things that cannot be explained by natural laws'.

I do not believe there is someone up there looking after me. However, I do believe that whatever intelligence created me, you, and every other creature on the planet, is a force for good rather than evil and intended us to enjoy our lives. I believe this, not because of an act of faith or because it would be nice if it were so, but because of facts I find impossible to refute.

MODERN, CIVILIZED, TECHNICAL MANKIND

… has only existed on this planet for the last 200 years. Yet we are so arrogant that we feel we know better than the accumulated intelligence of 3 billion years. Before you dispatch this little book to the waste-paper basket, let's examine some indisputable facts. Is it intelligent to create bombs so horrific that we daren't use them even against our enemies? Is it intelligent for half the world to suffer the misery of starvation, whilst the other half suffers obesity and heart disease from the effects of overeating?

POLLUTION

Is it intelligent to pollute our ponds, lakes, rivers, seas, the very food that we eat, even the air that we breathe? Is it intelligent to exhaust in just 200 years the timber and mineral resources it took 3 billion years to create? Is it intelligent to deplete this beautiful planet we've inherited and leave our grandchildren a world of desert and concrete?

I'M DEALING IN FACTS

Perhaps you're thinking that, far from removing your worries, I'm actually increasing them. Not so! You are just as aware of these facts as I am. They are part of the 'Ostrich Philosophy'. We try to block our minds to them, but they are like increasingly expanding black shadows forming at the back of our minds. They are a major cause of our worried state of mind.

LET'S LEARN FROM MOTHER NATURE

Perhaps you have also formed the impression that in order to be relieved of worry, we must first somehow reverse the effects of our stupidity. Desirable as that might be, it is not within the compass of this book. The point is that wild animals are affected more by our stupidity than we are. The pollution of the planet, combined with the destruction of their natural habitat, ensures that more species are becoming extinct on a daily basis. Ironically, we, the perpetrators, are increasingly worried by these unarguable facts, whereas it causes the victims not one iota of worry. Why not?

BECAUSE ANIMALS ONLY LIVE FOR THE MOMENT?

Undoubtedly this is part of their secret. Before I discovered Easyway, impending natural disasters caused me constant worry; nowadays they cause me not one iota of worry.

My dictionary defines worry as 'to be anxious about something uncertain or potentially dangerous'. The key lies in the word 'uncertain'.

GOLDEN RULE NO. 2

If you have a problem, actual or potential, first decide whether you have a solution. If you do, the problem is already solved. If you cannot find an immediate solution, devise a plan of campaign. If it involves seeking the help of friends or professionals, do so. If you are unable to solve the problem, accept the fact, but don't worry about it.

EASIER SAID THAN DONE!

Perhaps you regard **GOLDEN RULE NO. 2** as self-evident. It is. In fact, most of my advice is. All the advice I give is logical. You might well ask: 'If you have no solution to a serious problem, how can you do other than worry about it?'

I promise you, that it is possible not to worry about it. We all face very serious actual or potential problems that cause us not the slightest amount of worry. Let's first look at:

GOLDEN RULE NO. 3

You will find that if you analyse most of the things you worry about, they consist of problematic situations that might happen. Worry is always related to uncertainty. In the vast majority of cases, even if the worst happened, the result would be so trivial that there was no need to worry in the first place. We've been brainwashed to worry about trivia. Easyway is an exercise in counter-brainwashing.

GOLDEN RULE NO. 3: Before you start to worry, assume that the worst will happen and ask yourself if it is really worth worrying about.

INSTRUCTION NO. 2

What is the difference between **INSTRUCTIONS** and **GOLDEN RULES**? Golden Rules are the guidelines you need to follow when you have completed Easyway to ensure that you lead a worry-free life. Instructions are the guidelines you need to follow while reading this little book to ensure that you understand and therefore follow the Golden Rules. Still confused? Don't worry. There are only two instructions. The first was to open your mind. The second is to:

START OFF WITH A HAPPY FRAME OF MIND

How can I expect you to start off with a happy frame of mind when you have all the worries in the world weighing you down? You've obviously heard the adage: 'School days are the best of our lives!' If this is true, why do an increasing percentage of school children commit suicide? Because instead of school being an exciting and essential preparation to achieve survival and maturity, as it is in the animal kingdom, human education consists mainly of ensuring that during the most vulnerable period of our lives, we are not:

THE WEAKEST LINK

Why do we find this kind of quiz programme so fascinating? Are we all so sadistic that we actually enjoy watching doctors, psychiatrists and school teachers squirming before a hostess who makes the most evil interrogator of the Spanish Inquisition appear like Mother Teresa? I think not. I believe that quiz programmes are so popular on television today because we can satisfy our natural desire for knowledge in the safety of our own homes, rather than suffer the humiliation we experienced in the classroom.

GOLDEN RULE NO. 4

It is only the fear of appearing to be ignorant that keeps us ignorant. At some time in your life, you must have been at a meeting of adults being addressed by an expert on a particular subject. To you the expert appears to be talking pure gobbledegook. You look around and realize that everyone else appears to be as confused as you are. Then someone has the courage to stand up and say: 'Forgive me for being so thick, but I don't understand a word you've been saying!'

STICKS AND STONES MAY BREAK MY BONES

… is one of the first mantras we learn to chant, but we never absorb the beautiful truth of it. When that person does stand up, do we despise him? On the contrary, we envy him for having the courage to admit that he didn't understand. For him, it didn't take courage; neither does it for you. We've been brainwashed to feel ashamed if we don't understand something. That brainwashing is the greatest block to removing worry from our lives.

REJOICE IN ADMITTING YOUR IGNORANCE

Is that like saying: 'I'm stupid but proud of it'? No, it's the complete opposite. No one likes to appear stupid, let alone actually be stupid. It is true that some people are brainier than others, but every human brain is capable of incredible intelligence. What good are your legs if you are frightened to use them? What good is your brain if you don't use it? How can you remove ignorance if you don't accept you have it?

REJOICE IN REMOVING
THE BRAINWASHING

We've been brainwashed to worry. We've been brainwashed not to admit that we are ignorant and that we have fears and weaknesses. What is the only cause of worry? It is that our lives are not being controlled by ourselves, but by 'lady luck' or fate, or by our loved ones or our governments. I assure you that the incredible intelligence that has created each of us has equipped us to be in control of our lives and to lead a worry-free life.

ARE WORRY, PROBLEMS, STRESS AND FEAR SYNONYMOUS?

No! When you feel both physically and mentally strong, problems cease to cause constant worry, but become exciting challenges to be met and overcome. A powerful business executive regards his job as stressful, but where's the great stress? He knows where his next meal is coming from, that he has a safe and comfortable home to sleep in and that he won't be attacked by wild animals when he leaves it. The worst scenario is that he might lose his job. Is that life-threatening?

ANIMALS IN THE WILD
DON'T SUFFER FROM STRESS

A rabbit is subject to attack by foxes throughout its life; it isn't even secure inside its own burrow. But it is equipped with adrenalin and other drugs to handle this. It can feed itself and its family, and reproduce at a far greater rate than humans. The average rabbit looks far happier than the average human being. The only time a wild animal suffers stress is when it is imprisoned by human beings.

THE STRESS OF CAPTIVITY

We hate to see a caged animal pace its cage, it reminds us of the similar prison we have created for ourselves. We are the only species that forces itself to attend school and to spend half its life working for someone else. We are the only species that has learned to cry. What is the greatest instinct of all creatures? SURVIVAL! Why? Because our greatest gift is the sheer joy of being alive. We are the only species that has converted this joy into such a misery that many of us find suicide preferable to living.

AM I SUGGESTING THAT
WE RETURN TO THE WILD?

No! The modern world has too many advantages, such as freedom from starvation and attack by wild animals, a secure and comfortable home, fast and cheap methods of communication and travel. It is true that our brains are far superior to that of any other species: we should use them to make our lives happier, not the reverse. That is how Easyway works.

THE ONLY THING WE NEED TO FEAR IS FEAR ITSELF

I never understood the truth of Roosevelt's statement until after I discovered Easyway. What caused the Great Depression? It wasn't famine, flood or pestilence; it was the Wall Street Crash. In other words, over-optimism created by false economics, followed by panic when the bubble burst. Roosevelt solved the problem by restoring confidence.

GOLDEN RULE NO. 5

... is to stop seeing fear as an enemy or a weakness. Fear is one of the marvellous survival techniques with which Mother Nature has equipped all creatures to help them avoid injury or death. You should be no more ashamed of fear than you should be of installing burglar alarms and fire detectors in your home.

WE CONFUSE FEARS WITH PHOBIAS

Fear of attack, heights, fire, suffocation, drowning, etc. are perfectly natural and are vital to our happiness. Fear is like a burglar alarm: it warns us that we might be subject to injury or even death and enables us to take remedial action. Fear is a friend. A phobia is an irrational fear – a fear that has no logical basis.

DON'T CONFUSE FEAR WITH WORRY

Just as a fire alarm can be the warning of genuine danger or a false alarm, so can fear. If the danger is genuine, remove any worry by applying **GOLDEN RULE NO. 2.** In Western society there are very few genuine dangers that cannot be swiftly overcome. If the danger proves to be unfounded, there is even less need to worry about it.

COMMON CAUSES OF WORRY

Let's analyse some of these:

1. Being dependent on a person or an organization for something that we feel is vital to our happiness.

2. Feeling physically or mentally inadequate.

3. Worrying about our health or the health of someone we love.

4. A guilty conscience.

5. Agonizing over something that has gone wrong; crying over spilt milk.

6. Doubt and indecision.

SPECIFICS

Now think of a specific problem that is either worrying you now or has been a great cause of worry in the past. You'll find that it falls into one or more of those six categories. The mother of a deformed child, who smoked during pregnancy, could be worrying for all six reasons. Let's remove all six, not in numerical sequence but in reverse order of difficulty. **GOLDEN RULE NO. 6** is:

DON'T CRY OVER SPILT MILK

How many times have you used and heard this hackneyed expression, or its equivalent: 'No point in locking the stable door after the horse has bolted!' We acknowledge the wisdom in this sentiment, so why do we spend so much of our lives chastising ourselves for what's done? It's the 'weakest link' syndrome. We've been brainwashed to believe that making a mistake is some crime that deserves punishment and, if others won't do it, we feel duty-bound to punish ourselves!

IT MIGHT TAKE TIME FOR
THE PENNY TO DROP

The brainwashing has been persistent over many years and is deeply ingrained. Don't worry if it takes time to remove it. Rome wasn't built in a day. If you find yourself crying over spilt milk, rap yourself over the knuckles. You'll be surprised how satisfying it is to accept, without flinching, the sort of disaster that previously would have shattered you. You know it's stupid to cry over spilt milk, so train yourself not to do it.

REVISION

I didn't answer the earlier question: 'If you have no solution to a serious problem, how can you do other than worry about it?' If the disaster has already happened, it's spilt milk. If you fear it might happen, and have no control over whether it will or not, there is no point in worrying.

GOLDEN RULE NO. 7

Don't be frightened to make a mistake. 'He who never made a mistake never made anything!' Again, we appreciate the truth of this statement. Providing we act responsibly and reasonably, making a mistake isn't a crime. Ignorance is not a crime either; but we are at fault if we are ashamed to admit our ignorance and, as a consequence, do nothing to remedy a bad situation. Accept that making mistakes need not cause you to worry, and is an essential ingredient of a worry-free life! The key is:

TO BE IN COMPLETE CONTROL OF YOUR LIFE

How can anyone be in complete control of their life? A giant meteor could render us extinct tomorrow, as it did the dinosaurs. But that isn't life – that is death. It is the proof of what I am saying. If our greatest instinct is to survive, and our greatest gift is the joy of living, then what is the worst scenario we have to face? It is no longer to be living – to be dead!

DO YOU GO THROUGH LIFE
WORRYING ABOUT DYING?

Many people do, and very miserable lives they lead. Ironically, the only time I can remember worrying about dying was when it was least likely to happen – when I was a small boy. By the time I reached my late forties, I was expecting it. This didn't bother me particularly. Why? Because smoking had made me physically and mentally weak and my quality of life was so low that death was an acceptable alternative.

DO I WORRY ABOUT DEATH NOW?

Never! This is also ironic: the older I get, and the closer it comes, the more precious each day seems. I now feel both physically and mentally strong. I've learned not to waste those precious days crying over spilt milk or worrying about things over which I have no control or that might never happen. Why don't I worry about my impending death? For the same reason, I don't worry that a fortnight's holiday will end. Some people do. I concentrate on trying to enjoy every precious moment.

BUT IS DEATH THE WORST POSSIBLE SCENARIO?

Perhaps you can imagine something worse. So can I. But there is always the choice of death. Therefore death is the worst possible scenario. However, perhaps suicide is against your religion: that's your choice. Mother Nature is compassionate. Personally, I find it difficult to believe that the same creator who granted me the most precious gift of life would deny me relief if, for whatever reason, that life became intolerable.

HOW CAN THE DEATH OF YOUR CHILD BE WORRY-FREE?

I do not offer a tragedy-free life or assume that your life will be all honey and roses. Tragedies are inevitable, whether or not they are caused by the death of a loved one. But do not confuse mourning with worrying. Mourning enables us to absorb the effects of a tragedy, just as crying is both evidence of a tragedy and part of the healing process – don't we all feel better after a good cry? We know that it's possible to overdo it, but that's masochism not mourning!

IS THE KEY TO LIVE FOR THE MOMENT?

On the contrary: the main reason that most people's lives are so filled with worry is because they have lived for the moment. You can't enjoy a fabulous holiday unless you plan it and earn enough money to pay for it. You can enjoy the holiday itself, the anticipation of it and even the work you do to earn it. The more enjoyable the holiday, the more miserable you can feel on the Monday morning back at work after it:

DON'T RUIN THAT HOLIDAY

... by bemoaning the fact that it's over. By doing so, you would merely be converting a wonderful experience into spilt milk. If there's no point in crying over spilt milk, there's certainly no point in crying when none has been spilt. This is an example of when it's essential to think positively. You have a choice: either to wallow in that misery or to reflect on the wonderful time you had and enjoy planning the next holiday.

YOU ONLY GET OUT OF LIFE
WHAT YOU PUT IN

Another hackneyed phrase, but one that is only partly true. Like the holiday, you only get it if you plan and earn it. Wild animals teach their offspring the lessons they need to learn in order to mature and lead a happy life. Put in the right effort and you'll get out a million times more.

GOLDEN RULE NO. 8 is: Invest in the future. An obvious example concerns money.

MONEY DOESN'T BRING HAPPINESS

Usually quoted by people who haven't got it, this old adage has more than a grain of truth in it. In most cases, money increases the rich man's problems. He will counter with: 'I'd rather be miserable with it than without it!' Which is equally true. When I ask people to list their present, past and future worries, money is at the root of the vast majority of them. This is so, even when the worry concerns their children or parents, and even though the person being worried about already has enough money to keep them in their chosen lifestyle for the rest of their lives.

DON'T OVER- OR UNDERRATE THE VALUE OF MONEY

I spent most of my life as a wealthy chartered accountant feeling insecure, miserable and always wishing that I had more money. Since I discovered Easyway, I have about as much money as I had then, I'm happy, secure and realize I have more than my needs. I'm not being sanctimonious. If you are physically and mentally strong, acquiring sufficient wealth ceases to be a problem. If you are neither of these, you can still acquire vast wealth but you are unlikely to be happy.

YOU DON'T NEED MILLIONS
TO BE WEALTHY

What's the point of acquiring enormous wealth, surplus to your requirements, unless it brings greater happiness? So many people spend years working hard to acquire wealth, ruin their health in the process and find when they achieve their goal that they have no friends and get no pleasure from the things they can afford. Far better to reduce your expenditure to fit your income with a bit to spare and spend your life doing the things that make you happy.

DO NOT CONFUSE
RESPONSIBILITY WITH STRESS

I was brainwashed to believe that my job as an accountant was very responsible. Where was the great responsibility? If I made a mistake, was it life-threatening? It was certainly stressful, but that was because I hated it, responsibility had nothing to do with it. My present work is exceedingly responsible: a mistake could cost my clients their happiness or even their lives. Do I find this stressful? On the contrary, I love it.

BE CAREFUL WHAT YOU WISH FOR

It might be granted. Like myself, many people waste years trying to achieve dreams that they have been brainwashed to search for. It's like falling into a fast-flowing river and spending the rest of your life being controlled by its ebb and flow. I'm not advising you to abandon modern society, it has much to offer. But sit down and consider what you really want from your life. Don't at this point worry about whether you think you can achieve it. Make that decision when you have finished reading the book.

I DON'T REGARD MYSELF AS A GREAT WRITER

But rather as someone who has important messages to convey. In the Preface, I expressed my worry about whether Easyway would be successful. I knew it would work for any smoker, but was I competent to convey the important messages? I'm a perfectionist, very conscientious and I've just reminded myself of my responsibility to you. For a fleeting moment, I was worried that I would fail to communicate successfully with you.

WHY WAS THE MOMENT ONLY FLEETING?

Because I quickly reminded myself of one of the principles of Easyway: it's not a crime to make a mistake. Even if I do, there is absolutely nothing to lose. If I don't write the book, you can't benefit from it. I know it is impossible for me to achieve perfection, so I don't worry that I never do, but the attempt ensures that I do my best and leaves me with a clear conscience and worry-free. You can be blamed for not trying your best but no one can blame you for not achieving it, including yourself. Perhaps you are thinking:

THAT'S ALL VERY WELL FOR ALLEN CARR!

It's fine for him to have a clear conscience and be worry-free, but what if he fails to get his message across? I am happy to remind you that you are in exactly the same position – in an absolutely nothing-to-lose situation. Let me also remind you of **INSTRUCTION NO. 2: START WITH A HAPPY FRAME OF MIND!** Are you in a happy frame of mind? If not, why not?

IS IT SUCH A BAD DEAL?

After all, you have absolutely nothing to lose. You can take my word for it, a worry-free life is a truly wonderful prospect. Perhaps that is your problem – it's only a prospect. No, it isn't. Life was intended to be that way. For over 99.9999 percent of the creatures on this planet, it is that way. It's only the supposedly most intelligent species that creates worry. Let's test it out.

DOES YOUR DOG EVER WORRY?

The answer is undoubtedly, Yes. It worries when feeding time or walkies is overdue. It worries when you won't allow it to get at a bitch that is on heat. It worries when you are clearly annoyed at it for contravening one of your rules. But most of all, it worries when it is deprived of the company of the person whom it most loves and is dependent upon for love, not knowing for certain if or when that person will return. Your dog's worries are caused by his dependence on you. That's why he is so pleased to see you after a prolonged absence.

DOES YOUR PET CAT EVER WORRY?

I would say, No. I came to this conclusion after leaving my warm bed on a frosty night to admit through the front door a complaining stray cat that a week earlier had decided our house would be quite suitable for her purposes. I'd installed a cat-flap in the back door, but that had been disdained for the greater pleasure of keeping me waiting while she made a leisurely entrance, tail stuck in the air. I was convinced that her life was free of worry.

FREEDOM FROM WORRY

... is being in control. Not being dependent upon someone else for what we regard as the essentials of life. These would include sufficient time and money for entertainment, sports and hobbies. It also involves accepting and not worrying about potential disasters over which you have absolutely no control. A common source of worry that is harder to remove is:

SOMEONE DEPENDENT UPON YOU

Perhaps the worst scenario is a single parent with a seriously handicapped child worrying about what will become of the child if they die first. I am not saying that it is possible for anyone to go through life free of unpleasant experiences; what I am saying is that there is never a need to worry about such disasters, either by anticipating that they might happen, or even after they have happened. Let's consider some examples:

PUTTING YOUR DOG IN KENNELS

You need a holiday and have no choice but to entrust your pet to a kennel. You have a decision to make: either to take the holiday and accept that it will pine, or to forfeit the holiday. Don't confuse thinking with worrying. Until you've decided, you've neither lost the holiday nor caused your dog to pine, so there is no need to worry. The moment you make the decision, either you lose your holiday or your pet pines, to mope about either is to cry over spilt milk. It would be sheer stupidity to ruin your holiday by worrying about your pet pining. Don't do it!

BUT SURELY MAKING DECISIONS IS WORRYING?

Only if you are frightened of making the wrong decision. We've already dealt with this! It's only doubt and uncertainty that cause worry, in other words: **NOT MAKING DECISIONS**. We've also dealt with this. Weigh up the pros and cons, seek whatever extra information you need and, if the correct decision is not obvious, this means it probably doesn't matter much either way. If the decision turns out to be a disaster, there's no point in chastising yourself or crying over spilt milk. Put it down to the learning process and avoid making the same mistake in future.

HOW CAN YOU AVOID WORRYING ABOUT PAIN?

You might find the distinction difficult to grasp, but we don't actually worry about pain when we have it. Ironically, if it is severe enough, it stops us worrying about other things. I've been suffering severe toothache for a week. I'm a physical coward and find the pain extremely unpleasant and distracting. But I'm not worrying about it. I've already taken the action to solve the problem by making a dental appointment. In the meantime, I have no choice but to accept the unpleasantness and no way am I going to make it worse by worrying about it.

IT IS POSSIBLE TO WORRY ABOUT PAIN

Before Easyway, I would actually suffer severe toothache for months because I was worried about visiting the dentist. Why did I subject myself to prolonged pain and worrying when the actual treatment was virtually painless? I'd been brainwashed. I used to worry that prolonged, unexplained pains were caused by cancer. They never were, so why did I torture myself by worrying about them? Because it might have been cancer? True, but would the worrying have helped?

THE COUPLE I KNOW

The husband couldn't handle his wife's unfaithfulness and left the marital home. He resorted to the bottle and now appears to be about as happy as that sad cuckolded clown, Pagliacci. I don't judge him. The wife is now responsible for everything. It is obvious that she is under a great strain and that the quality of her life has been affected. But she remains cheerful. What can a mother do other than her best for her child while she is alive and make what provision she is able to in the event of her death? Having done that, there is no point in further burdening her life by worrying about it.

I THINK I'M A VERY LUCKY MAN

You might well be thinking 'It's all very well for Allen Carr to claim he's a lucky man. I could remove most of my worries if I had his money.'

Strangely, even when I was a street urchin, I never felt poor, and when I became a wealthy accountant, I never felt rich. I was only lucky in the sense that I discovered Easyway.

HOW DID EASYWAY MAKE SUCH A DIFFERENCE TO MY LIFE?

I believed that humans were physically weaker than wild animals. I also believed that I was intellectually and socially inferior to other people. Easyway didn't change my physical and intellectual potential, it merely allowed me to see that I had been brainwashed, and that I was physically just as strong as wild animals and infinitely stronger intellectually. That is **GOLDEN RULE NO. 9** and the key to a worry-free life. Easyway enabled me to realize that there was never a cause to worry!

YOU ARE JUST AS LUCKY AS I AM

The facts are exactly the same for you and every other human being. You've also now discovered Easyway and whether you benefit from it has nothing to do with luck. However, it has everything to do with whether you understand the Instructions and the Golden Rules and have the sense to follow them! **GOLDEN RULE NO. 10** is to ensure you turn the realization of your potential into reality.

MOUNTAINS BECAME MOLEHILLS

Before Easyway, I'd spent most of my life worrying about petty matters and turning molehills into mountains. When you feel physically and mentally strong, even genuinely serious setbacks become challenges to overcome rather than the final straw that breaks your back. Picture the strength of a tiger in the days before man – that's how I felt! Eighteen years later, now an OAP, I feel just as strong.

THERE'S NO SUCH THING AS OLD AGE

A child says, 'I'm seven-and-a-half.' The half is important: the child wants to appear more adult. Before we know it, we start lying the other way or wishing we were younger. We've been brainwashed to believe that old age is some form of disease. Animals don't count how old they are each year so they don't create this problem. If you feel physically and mentally healthy, it doesn't matter whether you are 2 or 92.

THAT'S A BIG IF

No, it isn't. We are made from the same muscle and bone as tigers. How else would we have colonized the entire planet, including areas with the most extreme climates? In my early twenties, I thought old age had already begun and, in my forties, I felt like a very old man. Was this so surprising? I'd poisoned my lungs and liver daily since my mid-teens and was at least two stone overweight through eating junk food. The miracle is not that I felt so lethargic, old and miserable, but that I actually survived at all!

THE STRONGEST MACHINE
ON EARTH?

It just happens to be your body. On average, it will survive for over 60 years, in spite of the fact that you will have abused it outrageously. Without such abuse, it would survive for over one hundred years, without breakdowns or the need for spare parts or maintenance. Why do we treat our bodies in such a cavalier fashion? One reason is that because our bodies are so strong they cope with the abuse, and we don't see any reason to change. But the main reason is:

WE OPT FOR THE SHORTER
BUT SWEETER LIFE

How many times have you heard the expression: 'But it's my only pleasure in life'. You don't need to be Sherlock Holmes to deduce that the person in question is resisting a request to cut down or quit smoking, alcohol or change the type or quantity of food they consume. A major part of the brainwashing is that we obtain great pleasure and/or a crutch from nicotine and alcohol, and that the only food that tastes good is the most harmful.

NOW YOU'VE SEEN THE CATCH!

Having got this far, perhaps you suspect that, in order to lead a worry-free life, you must give up drinking and smoking and live on a diet of fresh fruit and vegetables. Perhaps you further suspect that my ulterior motive is to hope that you will buy another of my Easyway books to help you do so. I promise you this is not so. If I were even to attempt to do that, I would be creating worry rather than removing it. I never even try to persuade smokers to quit, I merely make it easy for them to do so.

YOU DON'T HAVE TO GIVE UP ANYTHING

I only mention smoking, alcohol, etc. because they are a major part of the brainwashing process that makes us feel physically and mentally weak. We all know that we could enjoy social occasions and handle stress before we started smoking or drinking. We also know that non-smokers and drinkers don't need them. But to be worry-free, you need to understand that Mother Nature has already provided us with all the drugs we need to be strong and to both enjoy and cope with life.

CAN YOU VISUALIZE LIFE WITH NO SENSES?

Bad enough to be born blind, deaf or dumb, but imagine being all three and, in addition, having no sense of touch or smell. We regard fear, hunger, thirst or pain as evils, but they are survival alarms, warning us of danger, starvation or dehydration. Pain might be unpleasant, but it is also a warning that our body is being threatened. Our senses enable us to be aware of dangers and thus enable us to remove or mitigate the effects.

WE ASSOCIATE SOPHISTICATION WITH FRAGILITY

Drop your television on a concrete floor and it won't work. It is because our bodies are so sophisticated that we believe they must also be incredibly fragile. We regard babies as fragile, yet they are quite commonly the sole survivors of horrific car accidents. All doctors are aware that the most powerful healing agent is not the pills they prescribe, but your immune system. Your body will automatically supply you with drugs like adrenalin, as and when you need them, in the correct quantities.

MANY DOCTORS ARE WORRIED

Just as the obvious material benefits of the Industrial Revolution are now having to be paid for by pollution and exhaustion of the planet's natural resources, so many doctors are worried that diseases like smallpox, malaria and polio, far from being eliminated, survive in more virulent forms. Antibiotics also appear to lose their effect. We should not forget the vast majority of disease has been caused rather than cured by modern medicine. Are we gradually destroying our immune systems, and have you noticed that we seem to be discovering more diseases than cures?

OH, THOSE LOVELY PILLS!

I was brainwashed to believe that indigestion and constipation were normal. My doctor prescribed a pill and opening medicine respectively. Not until I was 50 did I discover that the cure was to alter my eating habits. The medical profession are the first to advise that prevention is better than cure, also that the chief causes of the leading killers like cancer and heart disease are diet, smoking, drinking and pollution, and are thus preventable. So why do we concentrate on magic pills rather than simple prevention?

HOW DO YOU ACHIEVE THIS?

It is obvious that it would be stupid to build a palace on a swamp. There are various essentials to leading a worry-free life: the first is to feel physically and mentally healthy. That is also the key that will enable you to achieve the others. How do you achieve this? Remember, we are born programmed to feel mentally and physically strong, and brainwashed to make ourselves weak.

PHYSICAL STRENGTH

There is no need to be an Arnold Schwarzenegger. We don't have to fight tigers or physically stronger people. In modern Western society, mental strength is key. But you are not likely to achieve it if you lack energy and feel physically ill. It's simplicity itself – just stop doing the things that make you feel lethargic and exercise sensibly.

DOESN'T THIS MEAN GIVING UP SMOKING AND ALCOHOL?

No, it doesn't! Nor does it mean you have to spend hours on a rowing machine. Make life easier, take up a hobby like running, walking, tennis, golf, whatever, so that you can not only enjoy the benefits of being fit, but also the process. There are many exceedingly fit people who both smoke and drink. But remember, most people who quit do so because they don't enjoy feeling lethargic and I cannot overstate the joy of feeling fit and worry-free.

SUPPOSING YOU WERE PHYSICALLY HANDICAPPED?

That doesn't necessarily prevent you from feeling fit and energetic. You have only to watch the para-Olympics to realize the incredible fitness that handicapped people are capable of achieving. Energy is a wonderful asset, far more valuable than money. 'Money doesn't make you happy, but I'd rather be miserable with it.' True, but that misses the point! What's so great about feeling miserable even if you have money? Energy makes you feel great to be alive, whether you are rich or poor; it will also help you to obtain financial security.

SUPPOSING YOU ARE BORN MENTALLY HANDICAPPED?

Some people are, and one of the kindnesses of Mother Nature is that such people haven't the intelligence to worry about it or the many other things that more intelligent people find so worrying. However, if you have the intelligence to read this book, you have the capability to become an intellectual giant.

FROM GOOF TO GENIUS

In my early years, I was often accused of being an idiot and believed myself to be one. Since I discovered Easyway, I'm occasionally referred to as a genius. Do I now regard myself as one? No, I'm the same person. Because I felt insecure as a youngster, I was influenced by the jibes; now that I'm mature and strong, I love the compliments I receive, but have no desire or need to kid myself that I'm other than an ordinary person. What I learned – and want you to realize – is that an ordinary person is someone very special indeed.

WOULD YOU LIKE TO WIN THE LOTTERY

… or be a champion? You already are! So am I and so is every other person on this planet. In order to be born, you had to compete with millions of other sperms to be the first in the race to fertilize that egg. We all have cause to be proud. Perhaps it did involve luck, but it also involved considerable stamina. Even Olympic champions don't have to compete against millions. We are all very special people!

WE CAN'T ALL DISCOVER EASYWAY!

I agree – I was lucky. But some people believe that there are fewer opportunities today and that's nonsense! As the rate of technology expands, so do the opportunities. It takes an effort for a baby to learn to walk and talk, but imagine its life if it hadn't done so! That initial effort is rewarded a thousand times over.

MY FAVOURITE CARTOON

… shows a young man on his first day at work in his father's business. The caption reads: 'This morning you'll start with Mr Jones, the export manager. I want you to pick his brains and learn everything he knows. Then, this afternoon …' Naturally Mr Jones doesn't look too happy. But the principle applies. When a top executive boasts, 'I've had 50 years' experience', what he is actually saying is, 'What I've been doing for 50 years I could teach you in three weeks!'

FINANCIAL SECURITY

... is one of the keys to a worry-free life. It is a fact that the vast majority of millionaires aren't financial geniuses who planned their careers. They are people who couldn't get a job and were forced to survive alone, or stumbled onto a good idea, or couldn't find work in their own village or country, or worked for someone else and thought, 'I'm sure I can do better'.

LEARNING

So many of us have been brainwashed to believe that we don't have what it takes, or are fearful of learning or frightened of making a mistake. If you want to do more with your life, realize that you have absolutely nothing to lose. See the accumulation of knowledge as it really is: an exciting and pleasurable challenge, an investment in a happier life. Start thinking about what you would like to do and what skills you need to acquire. Discuss it with your friends, and remember, the only people who are really stupid are those who are frightened of looking stupid.

YOU CAN'T TEACH AN OLD DOG NEW TRICKS

Yes, you can! **GOLDEN RULE NO. 11** is to accept that it's never too late to learn. For every hackneyed adage, there's an equally hackneyed contradiction: 'Look before you leap'; 'He who hesitates is lost'. I should have matured and taken control of my life in my teens. Was the fact that I didn't, a logical reason for not doing so in my late forties? Think positively: you have absolutely nothing to lose and so much to gain!

SURELY, I'VE CONTRADICTED MYSELF

I've stated that one of the keys to a worry-free life is to feel independent. That's true, but just as financial independence is achieved by having sufficient wealth, so companionship is achieved by having sufficient true friends.

NO MAN OR WOMAN IS AN ISLAND

Let's face facts. For the first few weeks of our lives, we have just one friend. To say we don't need her is ludicrous; we rely on her for warmth, comfort, security and sustenance. As we grow and mature, we become less dependent upon her, but that doesn't mean we become more independent. A friendless child will certainly not find school the best days of its life. Let's face it, we all need friends and my idyllic life wouldn't be so without them.

DOESN'T THAT MEAN I'M NOT IN COMPLETE CONTROL?

Of course not. All my friends are special, but I'm not dependent on one special friend. I used to have a problem finding just one good friend, and more often than not that friend would turn out to be not so good. Now I find my problem to be the opposite: my life is so full that I don't seem to have the time to cultivate additional friendships. How would you define a good friend?

SOMEONE WHO LOVES YOU IN SPITE OF YOUR FAULTS?

You would indeed be lucky to find such a friend. I would also wonder whether such a friend would be worth having. Let's reverse the situation for a moment. Supposing you were searching for something you needed, like a new car. Would you choose one that had lots of faults?

WHAT WOULD YOU LOOK FOR IN A FRIEND?

Someone you find interesting and amusing; with a pleasant disposition; who has interests and a sense of humour similar to your own; who doesn't put on airs and graces; who will listen to your problems; who will give you sympathy and comfort you when you feel miserable; who is always there to support you when you need it; who is always honest with you; and who genuinely loves you. Wouldn't you like several friends like that? It's easy:

MAKE YOURSELF LIKE THAT

Like learning to be financially secure, it takes some effort, but the rewards are even greater. That is not only the sort of friend you would like, it is also the sort of friend that everyone else on the planet would like. So if you can make yourself like that, it means that everyone on the planet would like you to be their friend. If you went to buy a new car, wouldn't you like to be able to afford any car you wanted? Friends are more important than cars. Wouldn't you like to be in a position to choose any friend you wanted? You can: **USE YOUR BRAIN!**

WE ALL HAVE FAULTS

... and no one's perfect. Don't take the attitude: 'Take me as you find me' or 'If you don't like me you are going to have to lump me!' Your family, friends and colleagues would find it so much nicer if you made some attempt to rectify your faults. But the really important point is, **SO WOULD YOU**. It would also vastly widen your scope in:

CHOOSING A PARTNER

I'm not talking about a business partner, but about a
girlfriend or husband. This was of particular concern
to me as a boy. The ideal was the TDH: tall, dark and
handsome – Cary Grant, Gregory Peck, Clark Gable.
I was an SFU: short, fair and ugly. In the days before
discos, it was a brave adolescent who was prepared
to walk across a ballroom floor to ask a girl for a
dance, because if she refused, so would the others.

SHYNESS IS A CURSE

No, it isn't! Just as fear is nature's way of protecting us from physical danger, so shyness and inhibition are our protection against humiliation. Hugh Grant uses it as a positive asset. The key is to realize that shyness is perfectly natural and that many other people are also shy.

PHYSICAL DEFECTS NEED NOT BE A HANDICAP

Young girls would claim that they'd choose character before looks – I never believed them. But test it for yourself: think of the people you admire the most and ask yourself if you admire their looks or their character. Being an SFU didn't prevent me from winning the hand of the most beautiful girl on earth.

SO WHERE ARE WE AT?

Once you feel physically fit and energetic, and have developed your knowledge to earn an income that makes you feel financially secure, provided you have developed your brain to make yourself an agreeable person and that you follow the **GOLDEN RULES**, you will have removed the vast majority of situations that give you cause to worry. This leaves only one major situation:

WORRYING ABOUT
PEOPLE YOU LOVE

This is a classic situation. You love the person dearly but, for whatever reason, they make your life a misery. This is a chicken-and-egg situation. If you can first become physically and mentally strong, the situation will be much easier to resolve. But how can you become physically and mentally strong while this person is making your life miserable?

DOUBT AND UNCERTAINTY
ARE THE REAL PROBLEMS

Talk over what is bothering you with the person concerned. You might well find that your own behaviour is part of the problem. If this resolves nothing, and you come to the conclusion that things won't change, you have to make a decision. Whatever decision you make, you must ensure you are happy with it, otherwise the doubt and uncertainty will remain.

HOW CAN YOU NOT WORRY ABOUT YOUR CHILDREN?

Is it just my imagination or do children nowadays cause us far more worry than we caused our parents? **GOLDEN RULE NO. 12** is to teach your children the principles I have detailed above, so that they quickly mature and become physically and mentally strong. That way, you'll have no need to worry. There are several other important aspects to removing worry created by those for whom you feel responsible.

IDLENESS AND BOREDOM ARE THE BREEDING-GROUNDS OF WORRY

Making yourself physically and mentally strong provides you with the energy and financial means to enjoy **GOLDEN RULE NO. 13** – to lead a full, active, productive, happy and worry-free life. You'll be so busy enjoying yourself, you'll not have time to worry. But isn't this a very selfish attitude?

NO, IT ISN'T!

CONSCIENCE MAKES COWARDS OF US ALL

I didn't understand the meaning of this saying when I was a child. If attacked by a bully, my instinct was to run and be branded a coward! Again, it was the doubt and confusion that created the worry. I no longer believe that my creator observes my every act and that there will be a day of judgement. What I cannot deny is that my creator not only blessed me with life, but also, whether I like it or not, with a conscience! **GOLDEN RULE NO. 14** is to accept that you have a conscience and that you'll be happier if you let it be your guide.

HONESTY REALLY IS THE BEST POLICY

This is **GOLDEN RULE NO. 15** and I promise you that crime really doesn't pay. A common misconception is that the way to make a million is to swindle your customers and underpay your employees. It's bunkum! Commercially successful companies provide quality products that people want, at reasonable prices, and back them with excellent service. The moment a business falls short of those standards, it goes into decline. These principles also apply in life.

PEANUTS ONLY ATTRACT MONKEYS

Every successful firm knows that its staff is its greatest asset. Unless you pay them what they deserve, and treat them with respect and honesty, you will lose your greatest asset. Criminals spend their entire lives either in the fear of being caught or in the misery of having been caught. As an accountant, I knew many very wealthy people who couldn't resist fiddling their taxes and, as a result, turned their wealth into misery. A clear conscience is a small price to pay to remove the worry of not being able to look people in the eye and not being able to sleep at night.

A COWARD DIES
A THOUSAND DEATHS

I didn't need a day of judgement. I soon learned that whenever I hadn't the moral strength to act as my conscience directed me, I despised myself. I also learned that the easy and worry-free way was to let my conscience be my guide and act accordingly. Provided you've done your duty by your children, parents, friends and pets, you should feel free to enjoy life to the full.

WHO NEEDS A WORRYING PARENT?

A sympathetic ear, a shoulder to lean on, some positive advice and assistance – marvellous! But hasn't your child got enough worries without being burdened with yours, or being made aware that he or she is the cause of your worries? You can be no bigger burden or worry to your children than to live your life through them and interfere in their lives. Isn't it every parent's duty to help their children be strong enough to leave the nest and lead full and happy lives? What sort of child would begrudge their parents the same privilege?

A THING OF BEAUTY
IS A JOY FOREVER

If you spent many years creating a beautiful work of art just for me, it would obviously be your intention that I extracted the maximum pleasure from it. You'd consider me somewhat ungrateful, stupid, insulting even, if instead of enjoying that pleasure throughout my life, I locked it away lest it get broken or stolen. All I would have succeeded in doing was to convert that precious gift into a worry.

LAST BUT NOT LEAST

You and I exist and because our brains and bodies are so incredibly powerful and sophisticated, it is unlikely that we exist by accident. I therefore accept that I was created. I deal in facts: I cannot deny that my greatest instinct is to survive, which means my life is very precious to me. I regret that through brainwashing and ignorance, I locked that special gift in a dark and dismal cupboard. But it's no use crying over spilt milk; I'm so grateful for the pleasure of the last 18 years and look forward to the future with confidence. If ever you find yourself worrying, read the Golden Rules listed in the Appendix. You've already won the lottery! Which brings us to **GOLDEN RULE NO. 16** – don't waste the most precious gift you'll ever get

BY WORRYING ABOUT IT!

APPENDIX: THE GOLDEN RULES

1. Think positively.

2. If you have a problem, no matter how large or small, and cannot solve it immediately, devise a plan. If there is nothing you can do about it, there's no point in torturing yourself by worrying about it.

3. If you find yourself worrying over a problem, ask yourself what is the worst scenario? Most times you'll find that even if the worst scenario should happen, it's no real disaster.

4. Ignorance is a major cause of worry. It is nothing to be ashamed of. Being frightened to admit your ignorance is. It ensures that you remain both ignorant and worried!

5. Fear is your friend. Just like a fire alarm, it is a warning to make you aware of danger and thus enable you to remove the danger or mitigate its effect. Most of our worries are created by fear and most of our fears by ignorance.

6. Don't cry over spilt milk. Instead treat it as a valuable experience to ensure you never repeat the mistake.

7. Don't be frightened to make mistakes.

8. Invest in the future.

9. Be aware that you possess the potential to be incredibly strong, both physically and mentally.

10. Ensure that you realize this potential. It's the key to a worry-free life.

11. It's never too late to learn.

12. Teach your children the principles of Easyway.

13. Lead a full, active, productive, happy and worry-free life.

14. Jiminy Cricket knows best: always let your conscience be your guide.

15. Honesty really is the best policy.

16. Never waste your most precious gift

BY WORRYING ABOUT IT!

ALLEN CARR CLINICS: UK & AUSTRALIA

UK
Stop Smoking Helpline: 0906 604 0220
Website: www.allencarr.com
Birmingham
Tel & Fax: 0121 423 1227
Email: easywayadmin@tiscali.co.uk
Bournemouth & Southampton
Tel: 01425 272757
Brighton
Tel: 0800 028 7257
Bristol & Swindon
Tel: 0117 950 1441
Email: stopsmoking@easywaybristol.co.uk
Cardiff & Swansea
Tel: 0117 950 1441
Email: stopsmoking@easywaycardiff.co.uk
Exeter
Tel: 0117 950 1441
Email: stopsmoking@easywayexeter.co.uk
High Wycombe, Oxford & Aylesbury
Tel: 0800 0197 017
Email: kim@easywaybucks.co.uk
Kent
Tel: 01622 832 554
Email: easywaykent@yahoo.co.uk
London
Tel: 020 8944 7761
Email: postmaster@allencarr.demon.co.uk

Manchester
Tel: 0800 804 6796 (Freephone)
Email: stopsmoking@easywaymanchester.co.uk
North East
Tel & Fax: 0191 581 0449
Email: info@stopsmoking-uk.net
Reading
Tel: 0800 028 7257
Scotland
Sessions held throughout Scotland
Tel: 0845 450 1375
Email: info@easywayscotland.co.uk
Staines & Heathrow
Tel: 0800 028 7257
Yorkshire
Tel: 0800 804 6796 (Freephone)
Email: stopsmoking@easywayyorkshire.co.uk

AUSTRALIA
South Queensland
Tel: 1300 855 806 (Freecall)
Email: sq@allencarr.com.au
Sydney, New South Wales
Tel & Fax: 1300 785 180
Email: nsw@allencarr.com.au
Victoria, Tasmania, ACT
Tel: 03 9894 8866 or 1 300 790 565 (Freecall)
Email: info@allencarr.com.au